SPIRITUAL TRANSFORMATION & GIVING

+Bishop Alexei of Sitka and Alaska

ANCIENT FAITH PUBLISHING

CHESTERTON, INDIANA

Published by:
  Ancient Faith Publishing
  A Division of Ancient Faith Ministries
  1050 Broadway, Suite 14
  Chesterton, IN 46304

ISBN: 978-1-955890-43-4

1

Giving to those in need as a natural expression of human altruism

*L*ord, have mercy. No prayer is offered more frequently in the Orthodox Church than this simple supplication. Mercy is the primary divine energy, activity, or action that we pray the Lord God will have on us and on His world. This describes perfectly how the gospel changes our own orientation toward what we have, which in turn reaches into who we are meant to be. We have what we have in order that we may be merciful stewards of God's own mercy toward us, acting with generosity to those in need and to the Church, which needs our collaboration, our synergy. In other words, the most basic prayer of our Church is at the very root of the virtue, the way of life, which is the chief characteristic of the Christian.

There are many ways to speak about this virtue of being merciful and compassionate, which takes flesh in merciful and compassionate behavior. The Greek term is *eleēmosynē*, a concept that is far too narrowly translated as "almsgiving." The ending *synē* bespeaks a frame of mind and the root of mercy itself—the olive oil base for that precious ointment generously poured forth,"Running down on the beard, / The beard of Aaron, / Running down on the edge of his garments" (Psalm 133:2).

Thus almsgiving is what the person who is merciful does. Making donations—in the simplest terms, giving money—is giving the wherewithal for someone else to flourish, for a community and a church to flourish, which is precisely what the mercy of God does for us all. For a Christian, being compassionately merciful, supporting the mission of the Church, and making donations to those in need is not an option, but a conviction about our very identity, once we have decided to take up our cross and follow Christ. From that point forward, we are to be "merciful, just as your Father also is merciful" (Luke 6:36). In doing so consistently and in the right spirit, the believer is transformed—purified, illumined, and even deified. All this happens through that synergy between our mercy and God's mercy, our effort and God's grace, for "nothing attracts God to us so much as mercy."[1]

Being merciful, giving alms, supporting the mission of the faithful is part of the process of a Christian becoming Christlike. But this activity has never been the exclusive property of Christianity. Some of the most magnificent moments of human kindness in history are comprised of examples of what psychologists describe as "costly behavior, . . . action aimed at benefiting others that involves some cost to the agent."[2] A biblical example is that of the centurion who was not a Jew but was known for his virtue, "for he loves our nation, and has built us a synagogue" (Luke 7:5). He used his money to show mercy and in turn received mercy from our Lord through the healing of his servant. Philanthropists like that blessed centurion can be found in every place and in every age, which means that giving to others in need or to worthy institutions is already a part of human behavior recognized by all as praiseworthy.

---

1   John Chrysostom, *Hypomnēma eis tēn pros Timotheon Deuteron* [*Commentary on Second Timothy*] 6.3 (PG 62.634).

2   Ayelet Gneezy, Alex Imas, Amber Brown, Leif Nelson, and Michael Norton (January 2012): "Paying to Be Nice: Consistency and Costly Prosocial Behavior," *Management Science,* Vol. 58, No. 1, 179–187.

If anyone needs to be convinced of this, St. John Chrysostom suggests posing a question regarding who is more beneficial to humanity, someone who speaks well or someone who gives to his fellow man.[3] The answer is nearly self-evident: being a merciful and compassionate steward in deed is far more valuable than being a skilled orator with speech, as actions speak louder than words.

In theological terms, we can understand this tendency to give as an expression of the *logoi spermatikoi*[4] present throughout creation, or as part of the natural law, or as basic strokes of the image of God still shining through humanity. We shall see, however, that Christian giving has its own fragrance, its own grace, and its own role that shapes the entire person in ways far deeper and far richer than does secular generosity—giving that lacks the specific intentionality that comes from the entrance of the God-man, our Lord, into our world.

Economists, sociologists, and psychologists may argue about whether generosity, falling under the larger umbrella term of *altruism*, is really selfless or is instead selfish and self-serving. But there can be no dispute that it exists in many forms and to many degrees. Obviously, self-serving donations, gifts, and offerings are not in keeping with the gospel of Christ and fail to transform the giver, who is so centered on self that his vision is not widened by the presence of the other. Our Lord referred to this self-serving form of giving when he instructed the faithful to "take heed that you do not do your charitable deeds before men, to be seen by them" (Matt. 6:1). This type of giving is not virtuous and does not lead to the Kingdom of heaven. Even in a secular setting, such giving is not without reproach.

---

3   See John Chrysostom, *Hypomnēma eis to kata Matthaion* [*Commentary on Matthew*] 52.4 (PG 58.524).

4   Justin Martyr, *Apologia Deutera* [*Second Apology*] 8 (PG 6.457b).

Through the lens of contemporary psychological literature, people become genuinely generous and altruistic when they make moral values a priority over self-oriented values and act accordingly.[5] This entails desiring to be better persons who open their hearts to others. The morally oriented individual finds altruistic people to be admirable and wants to be like them by forging a similar moral identity.[6] In such individuals, the values of honesty, compassion, fairness, and generosity are central to their self-understanding.[7] Individuals with a strong moral identity make sure their actions are consistent with their self-understanding, which in turn strengthens and reinforces that moral understanding of self.[8] For psychologists and Church Fathers alike, when hypocrisy is present, virtuous, moral giving is necessarily absent.

2

Giving to those in need is admirable and beautiful

In turning from the human generosity and compassion that are found outside the Church to the kind of generosity and

---

5   Hyemin Han, Jeongmin Kim, Changwoo Jeong, and Geoffrey L. Cohen (March 7, 2017), "Attainable and Relevant Moral Exemplars Are More Effective than Extraordinary Exemplars in Promoting Voluntary Service Engagement," *Frontiers in Psychology*.

6   Wan Ding, Yanhong Shao, Binghai Sun, Ruibo Xie, Weijian Li, and Xiaozhen Wang (May 28, 2018), "How Can Prosocial Behavior Be Motivated? The Different Roles of Moral Judgment, Moral Elevation, and Moral Identity Among the Young Chinese," *Frontiers in Psychology*.

7   Steven G. Hertz and Tobias Krettenauer (2016), "Does Moral Identity Effectively Predict Moral Behavior?: A Meta-Analysis," *Review of General Psychology* 2016, Vol. 20, No. 2, 129–140.

8   Americus Reed, Karl Aquino & Eric Levy (2007), "Moral Identity and Judgments of Charitable Behaviors," *Journal of Marketing*, Vol. 71, 178–193, 180.

compassion described in the Gospels and patristic literature, we are turning from morality-based human behavior to a theanthropic way of life. When believers donate their time, talents, and treasures to God and to the poor in a way that is divinely human, they are first of all looking at others and the world through Christlike compassion. They are then allowing the grace of that compassion to move them to action, which in turn further attracts the grace of God and widens the human heart.

Saint John Chrysostom considers giving to those in need to be a virtue higher than all the virtues, which means that it more perfectly encompasses and defines a person's moral character, and has the power to shape that character into the likeness to God, more than other virtues do. In a society in which asceticism was highly revered, Chrysostom was quick to point out that giving to those is need is higher than virginity,[9] fasting, and other feats of asceticism. Giving is greater than other individual expressions of piety because the benefits extend to many, rather than being confined to one person.[10] This means the virtue of almsgiving helps the person become less self-centered and consequently more mentally concerned with others, temperamentally loving toward them, and behaviorally motivated to help them. Almsgiving is also greater than any other virtue because it is at the very heart of the Christian way of life. According to the Fathers, almsgiving is "the mother of love, of that love which is the characteristic of Christianity."[11]

In like manner, giving to the Church and to others is even greater than working miracles or raising the dead. For in

---

9   John Chrysostom, *Hypomnēma eis to kata Matthaion* [*Commentary on Matthew*] 46.4 (PG 58.480).

10 See John Chrysostom, *Hypomnēma eis tēn pros Titon* [*Commentary on Titus*] 6.2 (PG 62.698).

11 Ibid.

giving, one is doing good to Christ, but in working miracles or raising the dead, Christ is doing good to us. Put a different way, when God works a miracle for us, we are indebted to God; but in giving what we have for others, God is indebted to us for carrying out His work here on earth.[12] Through our giving alms, Christ works in us; through us He feeds and clothes the poor.[13] Indeed, *work* is the operative word. "My Father has been working until now, and I have been working," our Lord once said (John 5:17). And Christians work as did their Master, showing mercy to those around them. The Fathers are clear: it is not enough for the mouth not to curse; it must bless. It is not enough for the hand not to steal; it must give to those in need.[14]

Saint John Chrysostom considers giving to those in need to be an art better than all the arts,[15] which means that giving is a way of creating and crafting something beautiful in the soul and of the soul. In fact, he calls giving to those in need one of the expressions of the beauty of the soul that is "not the result of nature, but of a deliberate choice and underlying inclination."[16] It is not merely good to give to the poor and to support the Church; it is also beautiful. Part of this beauty is intrinsic to almsgiving as a craft or art in which something beautiful is

---

12   See John Chrysostom, *Hypomnēma eis tēn pros Korinthious Deuteron* [*Commentary on Second Corinthians*] 16 (PG 61.516).

13   See Leo the Great, *Sermones* [*Sermons*] 19.3 (PL 54.188ab).

14   See John Chrysostom, *Hypomnēma eis to kata Rōmaious* [*Commentary on Romans*] 20.1 (PG 60.595).

15   See John Chrysostom, *Hypomnēma eis to kata Matthaion* [*Commentary on Matthew*] 52.3 (PG 58.522).

16   John Chrysostom, *Homilia exō euretheis Eutropios* [*Homily on the Banishment of Eutropius*] 17 (PG 52.414). "What is then the beauty of the soul? [*Ti oun esti kallos psyches*] Temperance, mildness, almsgiving, love, brotherly kindness, tender affection, obedience to God, the fulfillment of the law, righteousness, contrition of heart. These things are the beauty of the soul. These things then are not the results of nature, but of moral disposition [*Tauta toinyn ouk esti physeōs, alla proaireseōs*]."

fashioned, beautiful like the cosmos itself. Giving to those in need is beautiful both in terms of connection to another and in terms of the value for which treasures are sacrificed.[17] The beauty of an inspiring act of charity makes a claim on us personally. We are humbled by its presence, which calls us to set aside all posturing,[18] to renounce all narcissism,[19] and to surrender ourselves to this beauty.[20] A moral act of beauty "lifts us out of everyday life and provides us with an occasion for transcendence."[21]

3

Giving to those in need is central to the Christian life

If giving to those in need, giving to the Church, or showing mercy is a spiritual activity, a kind of asceticism greater than other ascetic feats; if it is greater than the working of miracles; if it is the art of arts, fashioning the very beauty of the soul, it is not possible to speak about the Christian life and not include this aspect of Christian living in our discourse. The healthy life in Christ involves an ordered relationship of the believer with self, God, and neighbor, which is achieved primarily by three activities that define the Christian life: fasting, prayer, and giving alms.[22] We show a proper love for

---

17 Neeli Bendapudi, Surendra N. Singh, and Yenkat Bendapudi (July, 1996): "Enhancing Helping Behavior: An Integrative Framework for Promotion Planning," *Journal of Marketing,* Vol. 60, No. 3, 33–49.

18 Martin Schmidt, "Beauty, Ugliness and the Sublime," *Journal of Analytical Psychology,* 64 (2019), 88.

19 Roger Scruton, *Beauty: A Very Short Introduction* (Oxford: Oxford University Press, 2011), 145–146.

20 George Hagman, "The Sense of Beauty," *International Journal of Psychoanalysis,* 83 (2002), 669–670.

21 Hagman, 669.

22 See Leo the Great, *Sermones* [*Sermons*], 12.4 (PL 54.171cd).

self by disciplining ourselves with abstinence and fasting. We show the proper love for God by conversing with Him. And we show the proper love for our neighbor by sharing what we have through almsgiving.

Fasting, prayer, and almsgiving are also the chief virtues with which the believer can overcome the chief passions of gluttony, vainglory, and avarice, respectively.[23] By fasting, lust is extinguished; by prayer God is propitiated; and by alms our own debts are forgiven.[24] In terms of the aspects of the Christian life, fasting strengthens purity, prayer strengthens faith, and almsgiving strengthens kindness.[25] If one were to remove any of these aspects of the Christian life—fasting, prayer, or almsgiving—one would be left with a caricature of Christianity that would no longer be salvific.

Together, however, these three spiritual practices and orientations mutually support and strengthen each other. Some Fathers consider prayer and almsgiving to be the two wings that enable fasting to be profitable.[26] Others consider almsgiving and fasting as the two wings that help prayer fly to God,[27] causing those prayers to ascend more quickly.[28] Regardless of whether almsgiving helps fasting or prayer, one thing, according to the Fathers, is certain: without alms, prayer is weak;[29] with alms, prayer is greatly assisted.[30]

What matters most in prayer is not how many prostrations we have made or how long we have prayed, as important as

---

23 See *Opus imperfectum in Matthaeum* 15.1 (PG 56.715).

24 See Leo the Great, *Sermones [Sermons]*, 12.4 (PL 54.171d).

25 See Leo the Great, *Sermones [Sermons]*, 12.4 (PL 54.172).

26 See Severian of Gabala, *Eis tēn prōtēn hēmera tēs kosmopoiia [On the First Day of the Creation of the World]* 4.10 (PG 56.470).

27 See Augustine, *Enarrationes in Psalmos [Explanations on the Psalms]* 43.8 (PL 36.482).

28 See Leo the Great, *Sermones [Sermons]*, 16.2 (PL 54.177).

29 See *Opus imperfectum in Matthaeum* 2 (PG 56.642-3).

30 See Augustine, *Epistolae [Letters]* 130.24 (PL 33.503).

these factors are. What matters is our works of love toward others, which support those prayers.[31] In particular, giving alms increases both the faith in our heart and our confidence in God's presence,[32] which in turn makes it more likely for our prayers to be heard.[33] Alms are in fact a prayer that "calls to the secret ears of God"[34] and a way to meditate on the law of God.[35] And so a robust spiritual life is dependent on the quality of our prayer, fasts, and almsgiving. The more frequent the prayers, the longer the fasts, and the more liberal the alms, the more robust is the spiritual life.[36]

Another way of looking at the Christian life is in terms of repentance. In particular, the Fathers outline five ways of repentance: self-reproach for sins, the forgiveness of our neighbors' sins, prayer, almsgiving, and humility.[37] Like the various aspects of the Christian life, these ways of repenting are interrelated and mutually support one another. A Christian should repent in all five ways: turning to God through prayer, tending to self with self-reproach and humility, and

---

31 See John Chrysostom, *Hypomnēma eis tēn pros Timotheon Deuteron* [*Commentary on Second Timothy*] 1.4 (PG 62.604).

32 See *Opus imperfectum in Matthaeum* 15 (PG 56.715).

33 John Cassian, *Collationes* [*Conferences*] 2.21–33 (PG 49.1213–1214); Augustine, *Civitate Dei* [*City of God*] 21.27b (PL 41.747).

34 See Gregory the Great, *Registrum epistolarum* [*Register of Letters*], *Epistola ad Theodorum Medicum* [*Letter to Theodore the Physician*] 7.28 (PL 77.883cd).

35 See Jerome, *Liber de expositione Psalmorum* [*Book on the Exposition of the Psalms*] 1 (PG 26.1280c).

36 See Leo the Great, *Sermones* [*Sermons*], 71.1 (PL 54.387a): "*eleemosynae largiores*" ["greater alms"].

37 See John Chrysostom, *Pros tous legontas hoti daimones ta anthrōpina dioikousi* [*Against Those Who Say That Demons Direct the Affairs of Men*] 2.5 (PG 49.262): "(1) hamartēmatōn katagnōsis..., (2) to mē mnēsikakein tois echthrois, to kratein orgēs, to aphienai ta syndoulika hamartēmata. (3) Euchē zeousa kai akribēs, kai apo bathytatēs kardias, (4) tēn eleēmosynē (5) to metriazein de kai tapeinophronein tōn eirēmenōn hapantōn..., tēn tapeinophrosynēn."

loving others through forgiveness and almsgiving. It is a sign of our Lord's mercy that He carved out many roads by which a person can reach salvation: "If you are unable to enter the kingdom by way of virginity, enter it then by way of a single marriage. Are you not able to enter it by one marriage? Perhaps you can do so by means of a second marriage. Are you unable to enter by the way of continence? Enter then by the way of almsgiving."[38]

Clearly, for the Fathers, almsgiving is intrinsic to salvation. They go so far as to say that without humility and almsgiving, salvation is not possible.[39] Saint Cyprian of Carthage links almsgiving with the mystery of baptism as a way of intentionally putting off the old man and putting on the new in a way that touches the entire person.[40] The Fathers repeatedly make the statement that sins are pardoned because of one's generosity. The logic is simple. As Saint Augustine put it, "You give alms. You receive alms."[41] "Almsgiving is a work of love, and we know that 'love covers a multitude of sins.'"[42] Elsewhere the saintly bishop of Hippo writes, "You shall therefore go into the kingdom, not because you have not sinned, but because you have redeemed your sins by alms."[43]

Saint John Chrysostom makes this statement repeatedly

38 John Chrysostom, *Homilia exō euretheis Eutropios* [*Homily on the Banishment of Eutropius*] 15 (PG 52.40).

39 See John Chrysostom, *Hypomnēma eis to kata Matthaion* [*Commentary on Matthew*] 47.4 (PG 57.485).

40 See Cyprian of Carthage, *De opere et eleemosynis* [*On Works and Alms*] 2 (PL 4.603); see also Leo the Great, *Sermones* [*Sermons*] 49.6 (PL 54.305).

41 Augustine, *Sermones* [*Sermons*] 376.4 (PL 39.1671a).

42 Leo the Great, *Sermones* [*Sermons*] 7.1 (PL 54.159); Clement of Rome, *Pros Korinthious Deutera* [*Second Corinthians*] 16.4, in J. B. Lightfoot and J. R. Harmer, *The Apostolic Fathers* (1891; repr. Grand Rapids: Baker Book House, 1988), 51.

43 Augustine, *Sermones* [*Sermons*] 60.10 (PL 38.407).

in his sermons: "Do you see failure in almsgiving is enough to cast someone into hell fire?"[44] "Give up your wealth not that others may be fed, but that you may escape punishment."[45] He even makes the somewhat shocking statement, "Let us purchase salvation through almsgiving."[46] Elsewhere, St. John clarifies his meaning when he notes, "Let us not say that the kingdom may be bought with money. It is not bought with money, but rather with an unsullied intention that may demonstrate itself by means of money."[47] A mercifully loving heart for our neighbor that touches our own livelihood to the point of sacrifice is the way we "purchase salvation." This is the way our love of self, *philautia,* is transfigured into love of our brethren, *philadelphia,* and we in turn are transfigured into the very likeness of Christ.

If giving alms is a basic path of repentance, part of a proper relationship between God, soul, and neighbor, and intrinsic to salvation, then the refusal to give is one of the many paths that lead to damnation. Salvias the Presbyter exclaims, "Damnation is the punishment for riches improperly packed away."[48] Those who hoard may think they are saving their treasure, when it is in fact saved "for their own condemnation."[49] Failure to give is cruelty to one's own soul and a petition for God to refuse to give to the soul.[50] Failure to give to the poor or

---

44 John Chrysostom, *Hypomnēma eis tēn pros Timotheon Deuteron* [*Commentary on Second Timothy*] 6.3 (PG 62.633).

45 John Chrysostom, *Hypomnēma eis tēn pros Titon* [*Commentary on Titus*] 6.2 (PG 62.698).

46 John Chrysostom, *Peri metanoias* [*On Repentance*] 7.6 (PG 49.332).

47 John Chrysostom, *Hypomnēma eis tēn pros tous Philippious* [*Commentary on Philippians*] 15.3 (PG 62.291).

48 Salvian the Presbyter, *Adversus avaritiam* [*Against Avarice*] 1.8 (PL 53.183c).

49 Bede, *Super divi Jacobi epistolam* [*On the Epistle of the divine James*] 5 (PL 93.36c).

50 See Augustine, *Sermones* [*Sermons*] 87.9 (PL 38.536).

to the Church is contempt for the poor, contempt for the Church,[51] and ultimately indifference toward God, denying His teachings in action, regardless of what is professed in words.[52] When people do not give to those in need, the wealth they possess ends up consuming them and corrupting them.[53] Their hands become withered with respect to doing good.[54]

4

Why is it so hard to give?

We have seen that giving to those in need, giving to the Church, giving alms is a beautiful art, intrinsic to the Christian life, and part and parcel of salvation, while the failure to do so is directly related to damnation. Therefore, Christians should automatically and naturally be giving people. And yet the plethora of patristic homilies on this subject indicates that Christians often need encouragement to embark on the spiritually transformational voyage of imitating our Savior's giving, compassionate, and sacrificial example. Hence, the Fathers nudge the faithful by identifying the deceitful desires and wrong beliefs that make it hard to give. They then encourage the godly desires and right beliefs that transform the soul. From a psychological point of view, the root problem is egocentrism; from the perspective of the Fathers, it is sickly self-love, philautia, which generates a host of passions, resulting in a multitude of sins.

In psycho-economic terms, the cost to the agent or the

---

51   See Jerome, *In Malachiam prophetam ad Minervium et Alexandrum* [*On the Prophet Malachi for Minervius and Alexander*] (PL 25.156b).

52   See Gaudentius of Brescia, *Sermones* [*Sermons*] 13.29–32 (PL 20.941b).

53   See John Chrysostom, *Hypomnēma eis to kata Matthaion* [*Commentary on Matthew*] 47.4 (PG 57.485).

54   See John Chrysostom, *Hypomnēma eis tous Hebraious* [*Commentary on Hebrews*] 25.3 (PG 63.176).

sacrifice of what is valued is the stumbling block. People in general and Christians in particular want to do what is good and right for social or moral reasons, but they often are not willing to pay the associated costs.[55] Although it may seem cynical, some psychologists suggest that people are more motivated by moral hypocrisy than by moral integrity—they desire to appear moral and to maintain a moral view of themselves without actually acting morally and incurring the costs for doing so.[56] This weighing of the costs is why people may not help or may give only token help to those in need.[57] In terms of economic utility, giving to charity, the Church, or the poor decreases one's reserves and the usefulness of one's funds.

Social and interrelational factors that, in the right configuration and intensity, can encourage people to be giving, in the wrong order and strength can do the opposite. If people feel manipulated or forced into doing the right thing, they will likely react poorly and begin to justify not giving by minimizing the need.[58] Sometimes people doubt whether they can live up to their own moral standards, whether they have sufficient moral self-efficacy to follow model behavior.[59] And so, doubting that they can give, say, ten percent of their income to the Church or to charity, they end up not giving at all. Even worse, they may become resentful of being asked to give, because their inability or unwillingness makes them feel in some way inferior or judged by the more generous.[60]

---

55 Sonya Sachdeva, Rumen Iliev, and Douglas L. Medin (2009), "Sinning Saints and Saintly Sinners: The Paradox of Moral Self-Regulation," *A Journal of the Association for Psychological Science*, Vol. 20, No. 4.

56 Hertz and Krettenauer, 129–140.

57 Bendapudi, Singh, and Bendapudi, 33–49.

58 Bendapudi, Singh, and Bendapudi, 33–49.

59 Rullo, Lalot, and Heering, 2.

60 Benoit Monin (2007), "Holier Than Me? Threatening Social Comparison in the Moral Domain," *Presses universitaires de Grenoble*, Vol. 20, No. 1, 53–68.

According to the Fathers, an interrelated web of passions, especially fear, is what prevents people from heeding the call and obeying Christ's command to be merciful. Giving alms is difficult for some people because of their desire for money, even though that desire is considered unnatural, as money is not directly related to satisfying a natural need.[61] The desire to accumulate wealth is itself caused by vainglory and extreme laziness.[62] Having a large reserve of money can make people feel good about themselves, secure, and as though they need not work. Thus they are tacitly saying to themselves, in the words of the foolish rich man in our Lord's parable, "Soul, you have many goods laid up for many years; take your ease; eat, drink, *and* be merry" (Luke 12:19).

In addition to the presence of the passions, an absence of faith leads people to make wrong appraisals concerning the value of giving to those in need; thus, they decide against giving. Saint John Cassian says the root of the problem is faithless anxiety compounded by grudging hesitation.[63] Those who decide not to give to the needy or to the Church are unable to believe that they are *really* feeding Christ and that Christ will *really* take care of them.[64] They do not believe that giving alms is similar to a farmer planting seeds.[65] Being of little

---

61 See John Chrysostom, *Hypomnēma eis tēn pros Timotheon Deuteron* [*Commentary on Second Timothy*] 6.3 (PG 62.633).

62 See John Chrysostom, *Hypomnēma eis to kata Iōannēn* [*Commentary on John*] 74.3 (PG 59.403).

63 See John Cassian, *Collationes* [*Conferences*] 21.33 (PL 49.1213): "For no faithless anxiety [*infideles servandi*] for getting food will annoy him who piously distributes and disperses his wealth already consecrated to Christ and no longer regarded as his own; nor will any grudging hesitation [*moesta cunctatio*] take away from the cheerfulness of his almsgiving [*eleemosynae hilaritatem*]."

64 See Cyprian of Carthage, *De opere et eleemosynis* [*On Works and Alms*] 12 (PL 4.633bc).

65 See Severian of Gabala, *Eis tēn prōtēn hēmera tēs kosmopoiia* [*On the First Day of the Creation of the World*] 4 (PG 56.471a).

faith, people think about the expenditure but not the yield.[66] They think about themselves but not about God.[67] They justify their lack of charity by claiming that Christ's commandments are impossible to obey, not from a lack of blessed examples, but from their own mistaken belief that they could not possibly fulfill them.[68]

In other words, those not inclined to be generous to people and institutions in need let themselves give in to fears about family property, but not fears about salvation;[69] fears about providing for their children materially, but not about providing for them spiritually.[70] There is a fear of the near and uncertain future, perhaps a recession or depression (to use the very soft contemporary equivalent of a famine), but no fear of the hypothetically distant future of the hour of death.[71] The Christian forgets Scripture: "He who gives to the poor will not lack" (Prov. 28:27).[72] Faith is indeed the measure of all things: how much a person prays, how much he fasts, and how much he gives to others is a reflection of how much he believes in Christ and that His word is true.

---

66 See Severian of Gabala, *Eis tēn prōtēn hēmera tēs kosmopoiia* [*On the First Day of the Creation of the World*] 4 (PG 56.470d–471a).

67 See John Chrysostom, *Eis tous andriantas* [*On the Statues*] 15.16 (PG 49.162): "*Ezēmiōthēs chrēmata; eucharistēson, kai mē tēn odynēn tēn apo tēs zēmias idēs monon, alla kai to kedros to apo tēs eucharistias*" ["Have you been swindled out of money? Give thanks, and observe not only the pain that comes from the loss, but also the gain that comes from thanksgiving."]

68 See John Chrysostom, *Hypomnēma eis to kata Matthaion* [*Commentary on Matthew*] 21.5 (PG 57.485).

69 See Cyprian of Carthage, *De opere et eleemosynis* [*On Works and Alms*] 10 (PL 4.632c).

70 See Gaudentius of Brescia, *Sermones* [*Sermons*] 13 (PL 20.941d).

71 See Gaudentius of Brescia, *Sermones* [*Sermons*] 13 (PL 20.939ab).

72 Quoted in Cyprian of Carthage, *De opere et eleemosynis* [*On Works and Alms*] 9 (PL 4.631d–632a).

5

How to learn to be more giving

GENERAL PRINCIPLES AND SPECIFIC AIDS

One would think that simply pointing out what we have discussed so far—that giving is a divinely beautiful part of repentance, necessary for salvation, and an expression of faith—would be encouragement enough for a person to give. And in fact, when faith is strong and the desire to repent and be with Christ is fiery, everything in the Christian life falls into place, including the sacrificial giving and merciful heart that adorn the character of every saint. But fear, uncertainty, and being of little faith cannot simply be wished away. Believers also need help to strive for the perfection to which the gospel calls us all.

One place to begin is mindfulness of the perfection of the Kingdom of heaven, which Christians strive to inherit, and the nonjudgmental lovingkindness to others that Christians are called on to cultivate. First of all, when someone is making a rational decision about giving, he or she must have in mind as a much-desired goal the ideal or perfect state of the life of the poor, the beauty of a temple, or a Church program. In contrasting that goal with the present condition of the poor or of the Church, the gift of being a coworker and of bringing those in need closer in some way to heaven should inspire a desire to give. This connection is verified by psychological research, which finds that when an individual is distressed by the distance between the beneficiary's current state of well-being and the ideal state, the person will naturally be more predisposed to give.[73]

Judgments about whether someone is truly deserving or is

---

73 Bendapudi, Singh, and Bendapudi, 33–49.

to blame for being needy are misguided considerations that can make us distance ourselves from our brothers and sisters,[74] causing us to forget that "all have sinned and fall short of the glory of God" (Rom. 3:23). Instead, we need to have empathy for the person or institution that is in need of help,[75] to realize and emphasize our fundamental similarity with them, apart from any external differences.[76] And above all, we need to look at concrete people and groups of people, even as our Lord did in the Gospels, rather than at abstractions.[77]

Giving to those in need obviously has value for the recipients. The Christian who struggles with the prospect of giving his hard-earned resources to others requires some education. Christians need to understand the value almsgiving has for them personally, as an art producing something beautiful in their own soul. They likewise need to understand the danger and harm that follow from hoarding one's possessions and coveting the goods of others.[78] Then they need to have the will to give alms,[79] which is also the desire for their own will to align with that of their Father in heaven, who sends the rain of His mercy on the just and the unjust (Matt. 5:45).

The will itself can be strengthened in many ways—most importantly, by a Christian way of life that is all-embracing in the pursuit of the virtues and in the practice of the ascetic discipline prescribed by the Church. The other virtues support the will to give alms. When the fruits of the Spirit are

---

74 Ibid.

75 Wendy Liu (October 2008), "The Happiness of Giving: The Time-Ask Effect," *Journal of Consumer Research*. DOI: 10.2139/ssrn.1292548.

76 Bendapudi, Singh, and Bendapudi, 33–49.

77 Han, Kim, et al., "Moral Exemplars."

78 See John Chrysostom, *Hypomnēma eis to kata Matthaion [Commentary on Matthew]* 21.4 (PG 57.297).

79 See John Chrysostom, *Hypomnēma eis tēn pros Korinthious Deuteron [Commentary on Second Corinthians]* 20.1 (PG 61.537).

present—"love, joy, peace, longsuffering, kindness, goodness, faithfulness, gentleness, self-control" (Gal. 5:22–23)—the law of self breaks down, and the will to care for others becomes active. In like manner, the ascetic disciplines of prayer and fasting naturally help, as they decrease a person's wants, making that person less covetous and thus more disposed to almsgiving.[80] Once the will to give alms grows stronger, exercising that free choice is intrinsically satisfying. Studies have even shown that making a free choice increases activity in brain regions associated with processing rewards.[81]

And, of course, the will is strengthened by faith in Christ's words, which "are more sure than sight,"[82] faith that does "not worry, saying, 'What shall we eat?' or 'What shall we drink?' or 'What shall we wear?'" (Matt. 6:31), faith that thinks more of treasure in heaven than of that on earth, faith that thinks more of God than of self. Once trust in God is present in the heart,[83] once the fear of God is rooted in the soul, there will be not only the will to give but a divine zeal around giving.[84] The teachings of the Fathers are clear: when the knowledge of God is secure and unshakeable, then prayer, almsgiving, and righteous behavior become a way of life.[85]

Given that reading increases awareness, strengthens faith,[86]

---

80 See John Chrysostom, *Hypomnēma eis to kata Matthaion* [*Commentary on Matthew*] 58.4 (PG 58.563).

81 William T. Harbaugh, Ulrich Mayr, and Daniel R. Burghart, "Neural Responses to Taxation and Voluntary Giving Reveal Motives for Charitable Donations." *Science*, 316 (5831), 1624.

82 See John Chrysostom, *Hypomnēma eis to kata Matthaion* [*Commentary on Matthew*] 88.3 (PG 58.777–779).

83 See Augustine, *Sermones* [*Sermons*] 66.5 (PL 38.433a).

84 See John Chrysostom, *Eis tous andriantas* [*On the Statues*] 15.2 (PG 49.154).

85 See Severian of Gabala, *Eis tēn prōtēn hēmera tēs kosmopoiia* [*On the First Day of the Creation of the World*] 4.10 (PG 56.470).

86 See Paulinus and Therasia of Nola, *Epistola XXV ad Augustinum* [*Letter 25, to Augustine*] (PL 33.101).

steadies a wandering mind,[87] gives rise to pious thoughts,[88] illumines the heart, and guides believers to virtuous behavior,[89] the Fathers suggest meditating on scriptural passages that will encourage the believer to become a giving and generous person. After all, St. Athanasius the Great noted that constant rumination on the law of the Lord is a necessary form of spiritual exercise that should be practiced regularly, so that good thoughts might lead a person to acts of virtue.[90] And so the Fathers recommend meditation on the many scriptural passages related to giving to those in need, which St. John Chrysostom refers to as the "laws in the New Testament and the Old Testament set down about almsgiving."[91]

The Latin-speaking Church Fathers, such as Saints Jerome, Cyprian of Carthage, Valerian, and Gregory the Great, would select important passages worthy of meditation for their homilies and letters encouraging the faithful to give alms. From the Gospel, they would suggest reflecting on our Lord's words: "Blessed *are* the merciful, / For they shall obtain mercy" (Matt. 5:7); "make friends for yourselves by unrighteous mammon, that . . . they may receive you into an everlasting home" (Luke 16:9); and "give alms . . . then indeed all things are clean to you" (Luke 11:41).[92] From the epistles of St. Paul, they would stress the verse, "your abundance *may supply* their lack, that their abundance also may *supply* your lack" (2 Cor. 8:14).[93]

---

87 See Maximus the Confessor, *Epistolē Kōnstantinōi* [*Letter to Constantine*] 24 (PG 91.609d–612a).
88 See John Cassian, *Collationes* [*Conferences*] 1.1.14 (PL 49.508a).
89 See John Climacus, *Klimax* [*The Ladder*] 27 (PG 88.1116cd); see also John of Damascus, *Ekdosis akribēs tēs Orthodoxou Pisteōs* [*Exact Exposition of the Orthodox Faith*] 4.17 (PG 94.1176c).
90 See Athanasius, *Epistolae Heortasticae* [*Festal Letters*] 11.7 (PG 26.1408a).
91 See John Chrysostom, *Hypomnēma eis to kata Matthaion* [*Commentary on Matthew*] 50.4 (PG 58.510).
92 Jerome, *Epistola ad Eustochium* [*Letter to Eustochius*] 108.15 (PL 22.892).
93 Gregory the Great, *Registrum epistolarum* [*Register of Letters*], Epistola ad

Especially common in patristic writings are exhortations to meditate on two works from the Wisdom Literature: the Book of Sirach and the Book of Tobit. Thus, they would advise reflecting on Sirach 12:3: "No good will come to the man who persists in evil or to him who does not give alms,"[94] or Sirach 3:30 (RSV Catholic Edition): "Water extinguishes a blazing fire: / so almsgiving atones for sin."[95] From the Book of Tobit, the Fathers would recall first Tobias's instruction to his son on godliness in Tobit 4:7: "Give alms from your possessions to all who live uprightly, and do not let your eye begrudge the gift when you make it. Do not turn your face away from any poor man, and the face of God will not be turned away from you."[96] And then they would turn to the exhortation by the Archangel Raphael in Tobit 12:8–9 (RSVCE): "Prayer is good when accompanied by fasting, almsgiving, and righteousness. A little with righteousness is better than much with wrongdoing. It is better to give alms than to treasure up gold. For almsgiving delivers from death, and it will purge away every sin. Those who perform deeds of charity and of righteousness will have fulness of life."[97]

It is significant that the Fathers turn to Wisdom Literature in seeking encouragement to give alms. In the context of the Wisdom tradition, giving to others and supporting communities is part of a path grounded in tradition, founded on the fear of God, and leading to life, peace, and flourishing. To give of one's treasures to others and to God is to be wise.[98]

Theodorum Medicum [Letter to Theodore the Physician] (PL 77.884).

94   Valerian of Cimiez, Sermones [Sermons] 8.3 (PL 52.718a).

95   Jerome, Epistola ad Eustochium [Letter to Eustochius] 108.15 (PL 22.892).

96   Leo the Great, Sermones [Sermons] 10/3 (PL 54.166ab).

97   Cyprian of Carthage, De opere et eleemosynis [On Works and Alms] 5 (PL 4.606b).

98   Craig Bartholomew and Ryan O'Dowd, Old Testament Wisdom Literature (IVP Academic: Downer's Grove, IL, 2011), 19–30.

And this itself should encourage believers to give.

Alongside these scriptural passages to encourage almsgiving, the fathers also recommend the remembrance of death,[99] which has long been a tool of ascetics to maintain their ascetic discipline[100] and a means to repel the suggestions of the evil one not to give to those in need.[101] In this case, contemplating the hour of death reminds the believer that soon everything he possesses will no longer be his. This encourages him to put his treasure "where neither moth nor rust destroys and where thieves do not break in and steal" (Matt. 6:20).

Sometimes the Holy Fathers would also encourage Christians to give more by looking at the precedent of the Mosaic Law, which was not abrogated and is considered less demanding than the perfection of the gospel. This makes a lot of psychological sense. Helping behavior is automatically reinforced when people see it as normative, what *should* be done,[102] and also as achievable, what *can* be done.[103] From the outset, Christians would not view the example from Jewish behavior as being significantly different from or radically better than their own behavior,[104] which in turn would increase the likelihood that they would imitate such attainable, ordinary moral behavior.[105]

In Deuteronomy, the law states that the faithful children of Israel must not appear before the Lord for prayer empty-handed (Deut. 16:16). This means that praying without having given alms is a sin that transgresses that law.[106] As the Jews were able

---

99 Paschasius of Dumium, *Sententiae* [*Sayings*] (PL 74.393bc).
100 See John Climacus, *Klimax* [*The Ladder*] 6 (PG 88.796c).
101 See Gregory Palamas, *Homiliai* [*Homilies*] 12 (PG 151.153c).
102 Bendapudi, Singh, and Bendapudi, 33–49.
103 Monin, "Holier Than Me," 53–68.
104 Han, et al., "Moral Exemplars."
105 Rullo, Lalot, and Heering, 2.
106 See *Opus imperfectum in Matthaeum* 15 (PG 56.715).

to keep this rule of always bringing a gift or offering when they came to pray, so Christians can certainly do the same.

The Fathers would also encourage generosity by pointing to the practice of tithing, but they eventually stretched the boundaries of tithing to reach the sacrificial giving associated with Christian perfection. Thus, St. John Chrysostom advised, when a craftsman "sells any article of his trade, let him give the first-fruits of its price unto God: let him cast in a small portion here, and assign something to God out of his portion, though it be rather scanty . . . recommending a deposit of not less than a tenth part," adding, "let it be a law for all who gather their incomes in an honest way."[107]

The Lord did not abrogate the tithe, even in matters as small as a tithe of seasonings and herbs, but He did not yet consider it mercy or an act of Christian giving.[108] The Fathers further note that tithing was a given for the Jews, who would give tithes upon tithes, making it disgraceful for Christians not to give at least a tenth of their earnings.[109] With a careful reading of the law, St. John Chrysostom reckoned the tithe as being not ten percent, but between thirty and fifty percent once first fruits, firstborn, and jubilees were considered,[110]—not including the donations for the Levites, widows, and orphans.[111] And, of course, there have been Jews who have been generous beyond the tithe, such as the widow of Zarephath, "who thought more of satisfying Elijah's hunger than of preserving

---

107 See John Chrysostom, *Hypomnēma eis tēn pros Korinthious Prōton* [Commentary on First Corinthians] 43.3 (PG 61.372–4).

108 See Augustine, *Sermones* [Sermons] 106.3 (PL 38.626).

109 John Chrysostom, *Hypomnēma eis tēn pros tous Ephesious* [Commentary on Ephesians] 4.4 (PG 62.36).

110 See John Chrysostom, *Hypomnēma eis to kata Matthaion* [Commentary on Matthew] 64.4 (PG 58.615).

111 See John Chrysostom, *Hypomnēma eis to kata Matthaion* [Commentary on Matthew] 85.3 (PG 58.760).

her own life and that of her son."[112] The Fathers also note that the law does not bring the believer to perfection, but grace tears out the root of sin. So tithing, though good at a human level, is as far from the perfection of a Christian as "an eye for an eye" is distant from turning the other cheek. Christian perfection is not giving a tithe but giving everything to the poor and taking up one's cross to follow Christ.[113] And there have always been Christians who do exactly that.[114]

The Fathers have also found it helpful to reason about the nature and purpose of money. Saint John Chrysostom notes that money is not intrinsically valuable but valuable because of our estimate of it.[115] When a person gives money to help those in need, he is using earth to conquer earth, as a text attributed to the saint once put it so beautifully: "You received earth from the earth so that you might conquer the earth through the earth."[116] And so the Fathers advise: whatever God has entrusted you with has been given so that you can be liberal with the poor.[117] Its proper use is "to loose him that is bound, not to chain her that is free."[118] And in fact when used properly, it really becomes a possession—a permanent one—since "nothing belongs to each individual more than what has been spent on one's neighbor."[119] The Fathers even suggest that the Christian should work not so much to make a living as to

---

112 Jerome, *Epistola ad Furiam* [*Letter to Furia*] 54.16 (PL 22.558).

113 See John Cassian, *Collationes* [*Conferences*] 2.21–33 (PG 49.1213–1214).

114 See John Chrysostom, *Hypomnēma eis to kata Matthaion* [*Commentary on Matthew*] 39.4 (PG 57.438).

115 See John Chrysostom, *Katechēsis deutera* [*Second Instruction to Catechumens*] 3 (PG 49.237).

116 See *Opus imperfectum in Matthaeum* 15 (PG 56.719).

117 See John Chrysostom, *Hypomnēma eis to kata Matthaion* [*Commentary on Matthew*] 7.3 (PG 58.708).

118 John Chrysostom, *Hypomnēma eis tēn pros Timotheon Prōton* [*Commentary on First Timothy*] 7.3 (PG 62.538).

119 Leo the Great, *Sermones* [*Sermons*] 16.2 (PL 54.177b).

have the wherewithal to make an offering to those in need.[120]

Patristic discourses are rich in commentary on what it means to give to Christ in giving to the least of his brethren (see Matt. 25:40). They urge the believer to understand a request for help by the Church or by the poor as Christ the King asking something from the believer. Even if he or she is poor, the King's willingness to come to the believer and ask has made the believer incomparably richer. Understood from this vantage point, it is an honor and privilege to give.[121]

The Fathers also refer to almsgiving as lending to God. They ask the believer to consider the difference between approaching a judge who is indebted to us as opposed to approaching a judge to whom we are indebted; clearly, the judge indebted to us for our almsgiving to him will be much more lenient in his judgment.[122] The Fathers also suggest that when we encounter someone in need, we realize that we stand before an altar on which all can serve as priests, offering a sacrifice of praise to God.[123] It is also useful to consider what we would do if we were facing death and could avoid it for a sum of money. Who would not give that money to escape death? Through alms, one is buying off eternal death.[124]

Finally, the Fathers note that giving makes the lives of the giver and the receiver not just better, but even heavenly. The Venerable Bede would say that almsgiving "renews the

---

120 Bede, *Expositio in Actus Apostolorum* [*Exposition of the Acts of the Apostles*] 20.35b (PL 92.986).

121 See John Chrysostom, *Hypomnēma eis tēn pros Thessalonikeis Prōton* [*Commentary on First Thessalonians*] 3.6 (PG 62.415).

122 See Cyprian of Carthage, *De opere et eleemosynis* [*On Works and Alms*] 16 (PL 4.638ab); John Chrysostom, *Logos peri metanoias* [*Discourse on Repentance*] 7.6 (PG 49.332).

123 See John Chrysostom, *Hypomnēma eis tēn pros Korinthious Deuteron* [*Commentary on Second Corinthians*] 20.3 (PG 61.540).

124 See John Chrysostom, *Hypomnēma eis tēn pros Timotheon Deuteron* [*Commentary on Second Timothy*] 6.4 (PG 62.636).

recipient and makes the giver rejoice."[125] The generous may not consider the emotional significance of giving, but giving does provide some direct increase in personal happiness.[126] Being merciful is good for the soul. It is in fact "the virtue that makes all virtues profitable."[127] Even psychologists note that "prosocial behavior is an effective behavioral coping strategy."[128]

According to the Fathers, giving in honor of the departed benefits the departed spiritually.[129] Giving on behalf of loved ones who are alive benefits those loved ones spiritually.[130] And that good is not simply a temporal, this-worldly good deed. As Saint John Chrysostom notes, "in either life, it shows us glorious."[131] Stretching out one's hand to the poor on earth, one reaches the very summit of heaven, where Christ the King receives the gift.[132] Repeatedly, the Fathers note that what is deposited in heaven remains in heaven as "unspeakable wealth." The Fathers are clear that the benefit of being merciful is much greater in heaven than it is on earth, for earth is but a shadow of what is to come.[133] But the benefit is not

---

125 Maximus of Turin, *The Sermons of St. Maximus of Turin,* trans. by Boniface Ramsey, *Ancient Christian Writers* 50 (New York: Newman, 1989), Homily on Almsgiving 71, 175.

126 Liu, "Happiness of Giving."

127 Leo the Great, *Sermones* [*Sermons*] 10.3 (PL 54.166ab).

128 Caprara, Gian Vittorio, and Steca, Patrizia (March 2005); "Self-Efficacy Beliefs as Determinants of Prosocial Behavior Conducive to Life," *Journal of Social and Clinical Psychology,* Vol. 24, 2.

129 See Jerome, *Epistola ad Pammachius* [*Letter to Pammachius*] 66.5 (PL 22.641).

130 Cyprian of Carthage, *De opere et eleemosynis* [*On Works and Alms*] 18 (PL 4.616b).

131 John Chrysostom, *Hypomnēma eis to kata Matthaion* [*Commentary on Matthew*] 52.3 (PG 58.522).

132 John Chrysostom, *Hypomnēma eis tēn pros Timotheon Deuteron* [*Commentary on Second Timothy*] 1.4 (PG 62.604).

133 John Chrysostom, *Hypomnēma eis to kata Matthaion* [*Commentary on Matthew*] 23.10 (PG 57.319): *"aphatou tou tēs eleēmosynēs ploutou"* ["the ineffable wealth of almsgiving"].

simply merits; it is the joy of having fulfilled the commandments of Christ.[134] For a Christian, there is the double joy of
helping someone else and doing something to the glory of
God.[135] A Christian should think every day about whom he
can cheer up and help, to be a treasure, a granary for others to
be helped from.[136] And finally, there is the joy that comes from
the grace of God that we experience when fulfilling this basic
commandment.[137]

6

The proper way to give

There can be no doubt that Christians are to be giving, but
for giving to be transformational, it must be done in the
right way. Giving must be:

- » unconditional;
- » properly motivated;
- » cheerful;
- » liberal; and
- » consistent.

Giving must be unconditional. There are no conditions in
which it is not appropriate to give and no time in which it is
not convenient to give. Sometimes undergoing a trial, such as
being robbed or losing money in this way or that, makes people less inclined to give. But according to the Fathers, that is
the very time they should give more—for when a ship is about
to be shipwrecked, possessions that weigh it down are better
thrown overboard. Similarly, by giving to Christ in calamity,

---

134 John Chrysostom, *Eis tous andriantas* [*On the Statues*] 16.6 (PG 49.170).
135 Origen, *Commentaria in Evangelium secundum Matthaeum* [*Commen-
     taries on the Gospel according to Matthew*] 77 (PG 13.1725–6).
136 Augustine, *Sermones* [*Sermons*] 376.4 (PL 39.1671a).
137 Augustine, *Enarrationes in Psalmos* [*Explanations on the Psalms*] 38.24
     (PL 36.410a).

one will have consolation for the earlier loss.[138] This is also a way of showing thanksgiving in calamities that brings the grace of God even further.[139] Giving alms as a thanksgiving whenever anything unfortunate or unpleasant happens to us is a blessed practice. Saint John invites us to try this and see how it can transform sorrow into joy.[140]

Giving must be purely motivated. In Christian stewardship, almsgiving, and giving, one's motivation, which reveals the secrets of the heart, is critical. Almsgiving should never be done with the goal of being praised by others for one's generosity.[141] In psychological literature, almsgiving for the sake of praise is considered egoistic, in contrast with the altruistic desire to alleviate a need.[142] If the end is other than pleasing God or helping one's neighbor—if the end involves attaining rewards, avoiding punishments, or escaping personal distress—the motivation, and hence the heart, is impure.[143] For example, giving for political gain or a tax advantage is not giving but a transaction.[144] One indication that such giving is not spiritually beneficial is that when tax codes make giving financially more valuable, churchgoers who in turn give more also attend church less.[145] In other words, they do not grow in virtue and closeness to God but move in the opposite direction. Giving in order to gain prestige, respect, or friendship, or to avoid scorn for being miserly, or simply as a result of caving

---

138 John Chrysostom, *Hypomnēma eis tēn pros Thessalonikeis Prōton* [*Commentary on First Thessalonians*] 3.6 (PG 62.413–5).
139 John Chrysostom, *Eis tous andriantas* [*On the Statues*] 1 (PG 49.29).
140 John Chrysostom, *Hypomnēma eis tēn pros Thessalonikeis Prōton* [*Commentary on First Thessalonians*] 3.6 (PG 62.413).
141 Augustine, *De sermone Domini in monte* [*On the Lord's Sermon on the Mount*] 2.2.5 (PL 34.1272a).
142 Bendapudi, Singh, and Bendapudi, 33–49.
143 Ibid.
144 Ibid.
145 Sachdeva, Iliev, and Medin, 4.

in to social pressure[146] is not an expression of Christian giving but of pharisaical hypocrisy.

Giving should be done cheerfully. For the Fathers, giving is not "so much for the sake of the poor as for the sake of the persons themselves who bestow."[147] This can be seen in the emphasis not on the benefit to the beneficiary but on the disposition with which the giver gives. That disposition is to be cheerful[148] so that one's giving may be pleasing to God.[149] Otherwise, the sacrifice offered is blemished.[150] Giving to the Church should never feel like paying taxes, for taxes are paid for fear of punishment, whereas giving to the Church or to others is done out of love for Christ, a love that makes one joyful.[151] This is why assessments and head taxes are inappropriate from a spiritual perspective. If one is sorrowful after giving, the fathers even suggest that it is better not to give at all than to do so hypocritically without faith in God or love for others.[152] Rather than thinking one is poorer for giving or is doing others a favor, the giver should feel grateful and indebted to the recipient.[153] Giving is also best done without drawing attention to self, much

---

146 James Andreoni (June 1990), "Impure Altruism and Donations to Public Goods: A Theory of Warm-Glow Giving," *The Economic Journal*, 100, 464.

147 John Chrysostom, *Hypomnēma eis tēn pros Korinthious Prōton [Commentary on First Corinthians]* 21.6 (PG 61.178); see also John Chrysostom, *Hypomnēma eis tēn pros tous Philippious [Commentary on Philippians]* 15.1 (PG 62.287).

148 John Chrysostom, *Peri eleēmosynēs [On Almsgiving]* 10.4 (PG 51.266).

149 Jerome, *Commentarii in Amos prophetam [Commentaries on the Prophet Amos]* 2.5 (PL 25.1019a).

150 Basil the Great, *Horoi kata platos [Great Rules]* 29 (PG 31.992ab).

151 Maximus of Turin, *Sermons,* 71, 175.

152 John Chrysostom, *Hypomnēma eis tēn pros Korinthious Deuteron [Commentary on Second Corinthians]* 16.4 (PG 61.516).

153 John Chrysostom, *Hypomnēma eis tēn pros Timotheon Prōton [Commentary on First Timothy]* 14.2 (PG 62.574).

as Christ asked others not to make His miracles known.[154]

Giving must be liberal. Our gifts should be like the widow's mite, not "a glass of water out of the sea."[155] Saint Jerome even advises that alms should reduce the capacity of the one giving to buy luxury items for himself.[156]

Giving should be consistent. Our giving should not be a chance occurrence.[157] Studies indicate that consistency and liberality in giving tend to go together[158] and over time coalesce into an important part of a person's moral identity and prosocial orientation.[159] This offers scientific corroboration of the spiritual transformation the Christian recognizes in the heart.

When someone gives to the needy or to the Church, what matters most is not the size of the gift but the largeness of the mind,[160] the purpose (*tēs proaireseōs*) of the gift,[161] and the

---

154 John Chrysostom, *Hypomnēma eis to kata Matthaion* [*Commentary on Matthew*] 71.3 (PG 58.666).

155 John Chrysostom, *Hypomnēma eis tēn pros Korinthious Prōton* [*Commentary on First Corinthians*] 21.6 (PG 61.178); John Chrysostom, *Hypomnēma eis tēn pros Korinthious Deuteron* [*Commentary on Second Corinthians*] 20.1 (PG 61.537).

156 Jerome, *Epistola ad Eustochium* [*Letter to Eustochius*] 108.17 (PL 22.892).

157 John Chrysostom, *Hypomnēma eis tous Hebraious* [*Commentary on Hebrews*] 32.3 (PG 63.224).

158 Gneezy, Imas, et al., 186.

159 Reed, Aquino & Levy, 180.

160 John Chrysostom, *Hypomnēma eis to kata Matthaion* [*Commentary on Matthew*] 52.3 (PG 58.522): "*Ou gar tōi metrōi tōn didomenōn hē eleēmosynē krinetai, alla tēi dapsileiai tēs gnōmēs*" ["For almsgiving is not judged by the measure of what is given, but by the generosity of the intention"]; John Chrysostom, *Hypomnēma eis tēn pros Korinthious Deuteron* [*Commentary on Second Corinthians*] 16.2 (PG 61.513): "*Ou gar tōi metrōi tōn didomenōn, alla tēi gnōmēi tōn parechontōn hē philotimia krinetai*" ["For the love of honor (philotimia) is not judged by the measure of what is given, but by the intention of those who offer it"].

161 John Chrysostom, *Hypomnēma eis tas praxeis tōn apostolōn* [*Commentary on the Acts of the Apostles*] 21.6 (PG 60.170).

intention of the giver.[162] Someone with the mindset we have described will not make a token gift, though the gift be a widow's mite and though objectively it may not be enough to alleviate the need. Christians give with the heart and leave it to God to provide the increase. Secular altruists, on the other hand, engage in a calculus that rejects token gifts, because token gifts do not allow them to solve the problem.[163] Ultimately, the best way to learn how to give alms is to look to God, who is the primary teacher of how to give alms[164] and "who practices it without limits."[165] This presupposes that the Christian not only wants to give alms but wants to learn to do so in the most perfect way, in the most godly way.[166] When giving alms, the Fathers suggest that it is best for the person to have no one in the heart except the Person of God alone.[167]

Given the importance of almsgiving in the Christian life, the Fathers suggest making almsgiving into a habit. Much as our hand automatically makes the sign of the cross during our prayers, so when we see someone in want or when we learn that the Church has a need, we offer what we can to help. Psychologists note that when giving becomes habitual, it makes the decision to give easier and one's attitude toward giving stronger.[168] The Fathers, well aware of this aspect of human psychology, suggest setting up cues and times for giving. In terms of times, the best day to give alms is Sunday, "the day

---

162 John Chrysostom, *Hypomnēma eis to kata Matthaion* [*Commentary on Matthew*] 19.1 (PG 58.274).
163 Bendapudi, Singh, and Bendapudi, 33–49.
164 John Chrysostom, *Hypomnēma eis to kata Matthaion* [*Commentary on Matthew*] 52.3 (PG 58.522).
165 John Chrysostom, *Hypomnēma eis to kata Matthaion* [*Commentary on Matthew*] 71.3 (PG 58.665).
166 Ibid.
167 *Opus imperfectum in Matthaeum* 15.1 (PG 56.715); see *1 Corinthians* 16:2.
168 Sachdeva, Iliev, and Medin, 4.

on which we received all the blessings which we now have."[169]

Having a specific place where alms are given is also important. As one Father puts it, "not only in the Old Testament but also in the New it is commanded that every Christian put something into the alms box every week when he comes to pray, just as the apostle says: 'On the first day of every week, each of you is to put something aside and store it up, as he may prosper, so that contributions need not be made when I come.'"[170] In particular, the Fathers teach that we need to make an offering whenever we enter a church,[171] and we need to make an offering before praying in private. Thus, St. John Chrysostom suggests having a collection box near the prayer corner, so that we make an offering before beginning evening prayers. He also suggests having such a collection box near the bed, so that we may sleep with an easy conscience.[172]

7

The transformational nature of giving

Above all, giving to those in need, giving to the Church, is about transformation, about growing "unto a perfect man, unto the measure of the stature of the fullness of Christ" (Eph. 4:13). When people give to those in need, when they support their communities, when they support the Church, they change.

On the neurological level, brain systems associated with

---

169 John Chrysostom, *Hypomnēma eis tēn pros Korinthious Prōton* [*Commentary on First Corinthians*] 43.1 (PG 61.368).

170 *Opus imperfectum in Matthaeum* 15.1 (PG 56.715); see 1 Corinthians 16:2.

171 John Chrysostom, *Hypomnēma eis tēn pros Timotheon Deuteron* [*Commentary on Second Timothy*] 6.4 (PG 62.634).

172 John Chrysostom, *Hypomnēma eis tēn pros Korinthious Prōton* [*Commentary on First Corinthians*] 43.4 (PG 61.373).

social attachment and affiliative reward mechanisms are activated when people donate funds.[173] Along with the positive emotions associated with giving, people's behavioral repertoires increase, their preoccupation with self decreases,[174] and their sense of self expands to include others.[175] They become people for whom communion with others is a characteristic trait.[176] There are also findings that people who make costly donations behave with greater honesty than those who make token donations.[177] Helping acquaintances, donating to charity, and spending time with others, unlike purchasing costly consumer goods, are behaviors associated with happiness[178] and hence optimism, a trademark of a Christian outlook.

In an Orthodox Christian context, repentance means changing the eye of the heart, and almsgiving is one of the ways that happens. In terms of a penance for sins, almsgiving is considered superior to fasting, which is considered superior to prayer.[179] Almsgiving is thus the particular remedy to be applied to the spiritual passions of greed[180] and fornication,[181] both of which involve taking from others for the sake

---

173 Jorge Moll, Frank Krueger, Roland Zahn, Matteo Pardini, Ricardo de Oliveira-Souza, and Jordan Grafinan (October 17, 2006); "Human fronto-mesolimbic networks guide decisions about charitable donation," *PNAS*, Vol. 103, No. 42, 15623–28.

174 Caprara & Steca, "Self-Efficacy Beliefs."

175 Freeman, Aquino, and McFerran, 74.

176 Sachdeva, Iliev, and Medin, 4.

177 Gneezy, Imas, et al., 188.

178 Elizabeth W. Dunn, Lara B. Aknin, and Michael I. Norton, "Spending Money on Others Promotes Happiness," *Science*, 319.

179 Clement of Rome, *Pros Korinthious Deutera* [*Second Corinthians*] 16.4, in J. B. Lightfoot and J. R. Harmer, *The Apostolic Fathers* (1891; repr. Grand Rapids: Baker Book House, 1988), 51.

180 John Chrysostom, *Hypomnēma eis to kata Iōannēn* [*Commentary on John*] 34.3 (PG 59.197); John Chrysostom, *Hypomnēma eis to kata Matthaion* [*Commentary on Matthew*] 41.4 (PG 57.451).

181 *Opus imperfectum in Matthaeum* 2.12 (PG 56.643).

of personal pleasure. Almsgiving also soothes wrath,[182] redirecting anger against someone by expressing love for someone else. But it is much more than just a remedy for those passions and a medicine for our sins.[183] It is an important step in overcoming the tyranny of sin. When the believer completely rids himself of the love of possessing, sin has no more dominion over him.[184] Giving alms prepares a person to be able to stand up in the face of tribulation or persecution.[185] After all, almsgiving is what prepared Job to bear nobly and thankfully the deprivation of all his things.[186]

God gives grace to the humble, and God gives grace to the giving. If one does not give to others, the Spirit of God withdraws. This means the withdrawal of the grace of the Holy Spirit, which is God's gift of alms to us all. When that grace withdraws, we can no longer safely walk on the road that leads from earth to heaven.[187] Almsgiving tames the wildness of human nature, making people gentle.[188] It affects the heart, raising it to heaven, even as greed buries it in the earth.[189] It is part of the "single-minded striving after eternal life" that purifies the heart.[190] What cleanses the believer is, on the one hand, the compassion present in the giving of alms,[191] and on

---

182 Evagrius Ponticus, *Capita practica ad Anatolium* [*The Praktikos*] 63 (PG 40.1237b).

183 John Chrysostom, *Hypomnēma eis to kata Matthaion* [*Commentary on Matthew*] 41.4 (PG 57.451–452).

184 John Cassian, *Collationes* [*Conferences*] 2.21 (PL 49.1213).

185 *Opus imperfectum in Matthaeum* 31 (PG 56.794).

186 John Chrysostom, *Eis tous andriantas* [*On the Statues*] 1.10 (PG 49.30).

187 John Chrysostom, *Hypomnēma eis tēn pros Thessalonikeis Prōton* [*Commentary on First Thessalonians*] 11.1 (PG 62.461).

188 John Chrysostom, *Hypomnēma eis to kata Matthaion* [*Commentary on Matthew*] 21.4 (PG 57.300).

189 Peter Chrysologus, *Sermones* [*Sermons*] 22 (PL 52.261).

190 Augustine, *De sermone Domini in monte* [*On the Lord's Sermon on the Mount*] 2.3.11 (PL 34.1274).

191 Ambrose, *Expositio Evangelii secundum Lucam* [*Exposition of the Gospel*

the other hand the purity of the hope in God that accompanies the giving of alms and makes the believer's mind pure and spiritual.[192]

Almsgiving is one of the ways we can humble our souls,[193] for we place the needs of others ahead of ourselves. And the more humble one's appraisal of oneself, psychologists have found, the more likely one is to give.[194] Giving alms fills the soul with hope and demonstrates one's faith, so that one can be like a green olive tree in the house of God.[195] It is a "robe of loving-kindness, holier than a sacred vestment."[196] It grants a "great, a marvelous light"[197] and makes us more well-ordered, natural, and wise.[198] It furthermore confirms our beliefs with actions, enabling us to be victorious over error and heresy.[199] Giving to others is to life as a harbor is to traveling by sea.[200] It is a safe place to be, especially when the sea of life rages. Almsgiving is also likened to the "ladder fixed to heaven; it binds together the body of Christ." Giving to others makes men like God.[201] It makes the image of God in man shine radiantly.

---

according to Luke] 7.100–1 (PL 15.1813cd).

192 *Opus imperfectum in Matthaeum* 15 (PG 56.720).

193 John Chrysostom, *Hypomnēma eis tous Hebraious* [*Commentary on Hebrews*] 9.5 (PG 63.79).

194 Simone Schnall and Jean Roper (2012), "Elevation Puts Moral Values into Action," *Social Psychological and Personality Science*, Vol. 3 No. 3, 373–78.

195 Basil the Great, *Eis tēn hexaemeron* [*Hexaemeron*] 5.6 (PG 29b.109ab).

196 John Chrysostom, *Hypomnēma eis tēn pros Korinthious Deuteron* [*Commentary on Second Corinthians*] 20 (PG 61.539): "*philanthropias stolēn.*"

197 John Chrysostom, *Hypomnēma eis tēn pros tous Philippious* [*Commentary on Philippians*] 4.5 (PG 62.211–2).

198 John Chrysostom, *Hypomnēma eis tēn pros tous Philippious* [*Commentary on Philippians*] 14 (PG 62.286).

199 John Chrysostom, *Hypomnēma eis to kata Matthaion* [*Commentary on Matthew*] 88.4 (PG 58.779–80).

200 John Chrysostom, *Hypomnēma eis to kata Matthaion* [*Commentary on Matthew*] 52.4 (PG 58.524).

201 John Chrysostom, *Hypomnēma eis tēn pros Titon* [*Commentary on Titus*]

Good stewardship, tithing, giving, and almsgiving are all obviously good for human flourishing. Psychologically, people who give without moral hypocrisy become more prosocial, less preoccupied with self, and more honest. They have a more admirable moral identity and are generally happier. In the context of Orthodox Christianity, the believer becomes humble, kind, gentle, and hardworking. The giving believer becomes courageous in trials and wise in time of peace. And above all, his relationship with Christ deepens even as his relationship with all his brothers and sisters in Christ deepens. The believer finds salvation, and by example, he brings salvation closer to those who are touched by his generosity to the least among us—his generosity to Christ.

6.3 (PG 62.698).

THE RIGHT REVEREND ALEXEI (TRADER) has spent many years as a monastic in both Greece and America. Before his consecration to the episcopacy, Bishop Alexei served the Church as a lecturer in patristics, a Greek-to-English translator and editor, and a student of clinical psychology. He was consecrated to the episcopacy on January 25, 2020, and elected as Bishop of Sitka and Alaska in March 2022.

We hope you have enjoyed and benefited from this book. Your financial support makes it possible to continue our nonprofit ministry both in print and online. Because the proceeds from our book sales only partially cover the costs of operating **Ancient Faith Publishing** and **Ancient Faith Radio**, we greatly appreciate the generosity of our readers and listeners. Donations are tax deductible and can be made at **www.ancientfaith.com**.

To view our other publications,
please visit our website: **store.ancientfaith.com**

ANCIENT FAITH RADIO

Bringing you Orthodox Christian music, readings, prayers, teaching, and podcasts 24 hours a day since 2004 at **www.ancientfaith.com**